Even You Are a Freemason?

EUGENE MATZOTA

Even You Are a Freemason?

EUGEN MATZOTA

From the author of

„MASONIC ETIQUETTE IN THE NEW MILLENNIUM,'

and

„NEW MILLENNIUM MASONIC ETIQUETTE'

2022

Cover, DTP&Layout: Eugene Matzota

Even You Are a Freemason?, by Eugene MATZOTA

ISBN: 9798408608331

Imprint: Independently published

Even You Are a Freemason?, by Eugene MATZOTA

The Theosophical Society, Fellow,

Most of the following
is or could be true,
presented for building
in the Masonic spirit,
in no way to destroy.

Any resemblance to people,
facts, and parallel realities
is just accidental,
used in a fictitious manner
or induced by the author and reader.

DEDICATION

*I dedicate this book to those who have
already passed to the Celestial Chapter above,
but not before helping me begin my spiritual evolution:
Baronet Kapri,
Grady Adams,
and Marcel Schapira.*

*So, thank you,
those who have done so much for me,
and I wish not to disappoint you
anywhere you would be now...*

EUGENE MATZOTA

This book is based on
the author's Masonic experience
of about 30 years, the study
of many Masonic books,
the Masonic Codes of Conduct
of the Grand Regular Lodges of the World, many
documents from the Board of General Purposes to
Grand Lodge of England,
and articles published
in written or online media.

CONTENTS

I address this book
to those many who believe
that Freemasonry
can make people better.

The others, few,
who, with or without their will,
no longer understand any of the ideals
of Freemasonry, may also have
something to learn.

If only they want to,
if only they could...

This book goes beyond the Ritual...

Of course, the author offers us his decades of
experience, placing special emphasis on the
influence of these wonderful new technologies that
make this world a sort of friendly, bigger village.

There will be a lot of talk about communication,
interpreting communication, and, in this context,
about using communication for purposes
that are not always honorable.

The focus here will be on what we call *Social Media*.

The usage of the equivalent words 'Mason' and
'Freemason', with all their derivatives,
will be made according to their context.
Similarly, 'Social Media', 'social media' etc...

ABOUT THE AUTHOR

Born in Transylvania, in a family with a long tradition, as one of the founders of the Principality of Epirus in 1204, the ancient esoteric teachings attracted the author since childhood. Reading and practicing the Teachings, as well as Freemasonic initiation, made him try to become a better person every day.

He learned and practiced on his own what he could understand from a diverse, sometimes disparate, but highly controversial range of masters, such as Helena P. Blavatsky, Jiddu Krishnamurti, Rudolf Steiner, *or* Annie Besant.

Finally, his writings were noted and, since 1997, the International Theosophical Society, India, *has accepted him as a full member. He has published, among other things, three books on Theosophy and how to answer questions about life and human nature.*

Eugene Matzota is the author of several reference works in the Masonic field, including 'MASONIC ETIQUETTE IN THE NEW MILLENNIUM' *and* 'MASONRY, MY DISCREET LIFE', 2015, 'NEW MILLENNIUM MASONIC ETIQUETTE' - 2019.

THOSE WORDS THAT MATTER

Freemasonry appears in the life of every man when the time comes, and when he is ready.

This moment is not when the urge to enter appears, but when he feels that urge.

Eugene Matzota

If you Want to Enter...

There are words we cannot ignore, phrases that would open your eyes and, as the case may be, can close your Gate. Freemasonry cares about its values, which do not necessarily have to be yours, maybe...

Chances are that you, the one who did not go through the Initiation process, will even now be a kind of Freemason, because Freemasonry is already, from a certain moment on, inside you.

You don't necessarily have to post quickly on social media some pictures of yourself in which you ostentatiously wear a badge, diploma, or white apron.

No, not at all!

Why would you want everyone to see that you are a Mason?

Unfortunately, there are quite a few who do this, among those who entered Freemasonry through the back door, if there would be such a thing as that opposite Gate.

You can be a Mason, in a broader sense, without necessarily being a member of a Masonic Lodge.

This is true for those who live a Freemasonic life, just as others live a Christian, Jewish, or Buddhist life, for example.

Of course, this would only happen at a certain point in your life, when spirituality transcends the matter that overwhelms us with its presence, usually.

Nobody was born a Freemason!

There comes a certain moment in life, that moment when you have accumulated enough wisdom to act in the old spirit of Freemasonry, while serving intelligently, not blindly, the demands of the *Creator, the Great Architect of the Universe.*

There are some texts, taken from the old *Masonic Teachings* of about 300 years ago, clearly defining some requirements which we cannot ignore, I think. Here, any compromise only brings harm to Freemasonry and its members.

In my interpretation, the one who wants to knock at the Gate would have to pass some Tests, not more than three, but *decisive.*

Then he may or may not knock on the Gate.

If one of you who reads and understands, and at the same time agrees with what the words gathered in these Tests say, then he can go on quietly.

If not, that's it, we have nothing to do. It seems, even so, at first sight, that Freemasonry is not for him.

For now, maybe.

Maybe never...

But the world is big enough, so you can live without necessarily being a Freemason, right?

FIRST TEST - CHARGES OF A FREE-MASON [1]

CHARGES OF A FREE-MASON,

EXTRACTED FROM
The Ancient RECORDS of LODGES
beyond Sea, and of those in *England*, *Scotland*,
and *Ireland*, for the Use of the Lodges.

TO BE READ
At The Making of NEW BRETHREN, or when the
MASTER shall order it.

I.   Concerning GOD and RELIGION.

A *Mason* is obliged by his Tenure, to obey the moral Law; and if he rightly understands the Art, he will never be a stupid Atheist nor an irreligious **Libertine**. But though in ancient Times *Masons* were charged in every Country to be of the Religion of that Country or Nation, whatever it was, yet 'tis now thought more expedient only to oblige them to that Religion in which all Men agree, leaving their particular Opinions to themselves; that is, to be *good* Men and *true*, or Men of Honour and Honesty, by whatever Denominations or Persuasions they may be distinguished; whereby Masonry becomes the *Center of Union*, and the Means of conciliating true Friendship among Persons that must have remained at a perpetual Distance.

---

[1] This is just an excerpt. You can read the full document at the end of this book, in the chapter ESSENTIAL DOCUMENTS.

SECOND TEST - THE TEN COMMANDMENTS OF FREEMASONRY[2]

Masonry has its decalogue, which is a law to its Initiates. These are its Ten Commandments:

I. .'. God is the Eternal, Omnipotent, Immutable WISDOM and Supreme INTELLIGENCE and Exhaustless LOVE.
Thou shalt adore, revere, and love Him!
Thou shalt honor Him by practicing the virtues!

II. O.'. Thy religion shall be, to do good because it is a pleasure to thee, and not merely because it is a duty.
That thou mayest become the friend of the wise man, thou shalt obey his precepts!
Thy soul is immortal! Thou shalt do nothing to degrade it!

III. .'.Thou shalt unceasingly war against vice!

Thou shalt not do unto others that which thou wouldst not wish them to do unto thee!
Thou shalt be submissive to thy fortunes, and keep burning the light of wisdom!

IV. O.'. Thou shalt honor thy parents!

Thou shalt pay respect and homage to the aged!
Thou shalt instruct the young!
Thou shalt protect and defend infancy and innocence!

V. .'.Thou shalt cherish thy wife and thy children!
Thou shalt love thy country, and obey its laws!

---

[2] https://archive.org/stream/moralsdogmaofanc00pikeiala/
moralsdogmaofanc00pikeiala_djvu.txt

VI. O.'. Thy friend shall be to thee a second self!
Misfortune shall not estrange thee from him!
Thou shalt do for his memory whatever thou wouldst do for him. if he were living!

VII. 0.'. Thou shalt avoid and flee from insincere friendships!
Thou shalt in everything refrain from excess!
Thou shalt fear to be the cause of a stain on thy memory!

VIII. O.'. Thou shalt allow no passions to become thy master!
Thou shalt make the passions of others profitable lessons to thyself!
Thou shalt be indulgent to error!

IX. .'. Thou shalt hear much: Thou shalt speak little: Thou shalt act well!
Thou shalt forget injuries!
Thou shalt render good for evil!

Thou shalt not misuse either thy strength or thy superiority!
X. O.'. Thou shalt study to know men; that thereby thou mayest learn to know thyself!
Thou shalt ever seek after virtue!
Thou shalt be just!
Thou shalt avoid idleness!

But the great commandment of Masonry is this: 'A new commandment give I unto you: that ye love one another! He that saith he is in the light, and hateth his brother, remaineth still in the darkness.'

Albert Pike, Morals and dogma of the ancient and accepted Scottish Rite of Freemasonry, 1871[3]

---

[3] Pike, Albert, *Morals and Dogma*, 1871, p. 17-18

THIRD TEST - BASIC PRINCIPLES FOR GRAND LODGE RECOGNITION[4]

Accepted by the Grand Lodge, September 4, 1929

The M.W. The Grand Master having expressed a desire that the Board would draw up a statement of the Basic Principles on which this Grand Lodge could be invited to recognize any Grand Lodge applying for recognition by the English Jurisdiction, the Board of General Purposes has gladly complied. The result, as follows, has been approved by the Grand Master and it will form the basis of a questionnaire to be forwarded in future to each Jurisdiction requesting English recognition. The Board desires that not only such bodies but the Brethren generally throughout the Grand Master's Jurisdiction shall be fully informed as to those Basic Principles of Freemasonry for which the Grand Lodge of England has stood throughout its history

1. Regularity of origin; i.e. each Grand Lodge shall have been established lawfully by a duly recognized Grand Lodge or by three or more regularly constituted Lodges.

2. That a belief in the G.A.O.T.U. and His revealed will shall be an essential qualification for membership.

3. That all Initiates shall take their Obligation on or in full view of the open Volume of the Sacred Law, by which is meant the revelation from above which is binding on the conscience of the particular individual who is being initiated.

4. That the membership of the Grand Lodge and individual Lodges shall be composed exclusively of men; and that each Grand Lodge shall have no Masonic intercourse of any kind with mixed Lodges or bodies which admit women to membership.

[...]

---

[4] This is just an excerpt. You can read the full document at the end of this book, in the chapter ESSENTIAL DOCUMENTS.

THINGS TO REMEMBER

Chances are that you, the one who did not go
through the Initiation process, will even now
be a kind of Freemason, because Freemasonry
is already, from a certain moment on, inside
you.

You can be a Mason, in a broader sense, without
necessarily being a member of a Masonic
Lodge.

Nobody was born a Freemason!

But the world is big enough, so you can live
without necessarily being a Freemason, right?

AM I THE ONLY ONE?

Am I the only one who Wants More?

What do I mean by that? Isn't it enough that we see each other at the Temple? Isn't it enough that we have to learn by heart those texts that are so old and cumbersome?

What more do we need?

It's been a while since I published, in 2013, 'MASONIC ETIQUETTE CODE', a book that reached many Brethren, not as many as I would have liked, namely, to all of them

Then came, in 2015, the publication of a new edition, which appeared in Madrid, 'MASONIC ETIQUETTE IN THE NEW MILLENNIUM.' With this book, I thought of offering to those who come after me on the hard Path of Masonic perfection some of what I experienced as a Mason for over 20 years ago.

Meanwhile, in 2019, I published 'NEW MILLENNIUM MASONIC ETIQUETTE', which is just another attempt to help those who want to be helped to behave like true Masons.

To me, publishing the first edition of the first book of Masonic etiquette meant a book written from the despair of a man who powerlessly witnessed the dissolution of values in society. I saw then, the same trend in Freemasonry, which is a mirror of society.

Now, almost ten years later, I find with great regret that even today, things are not at all as they should be.

Some more experienced Masons may not find many new things here, but I am not addressing them in the first place, but to those who have not yet found the Light.

I believe that openness to the profane world, the world of the uninitiated, must exist.

I wrote this book more for those who have recently come on this Path. It is a good start for those who have not gone through the Initiation process. Any kind of Internet search might not satisfy their curiosity.

THIS BOOK IS FOR YOU, TOO!

I must specify that, following the precise rules of discretion of the Order, I dedicated the book mainly to my Brethren.

Therefore, the author assumes no responsibility for any misinterpretations by the uninitiated.

All those who have not gone through the Initiation process do not master and, therefore, have no way of understanding different notions, rituals, and rules specific to the Masonic Order.

They should know what the massive distribution of stupidity means.

In other words: *fake news.*

I will try to help the profanes to understand more revealing nothing that is reserved for the Initiate. Therefore, I will address in more detail the influence of the Internet, which can be both good and bad at the same time.

The Internet is a miracle nowadays; it is not something that has always existed.

This miracle, which we can no longer properly appreciate because we believe that this has always been the case, allows us incredibly simple access to information. We must say that this is normal.

Internet=Highway to Hell?

it should be quite easy to understand that, if you have easy access to any kind of information, good and bad, this means that you have also access to a highway to Hell.

Not everyone can understand the dangers of false or falsified information.

Openness to the profanes has existed since the end of the twentieth century, but the Internet has been a real trigger for the process.

The entire Internet is indeed the place where we can see all the possible nonsense about Freemasonry. It may be just stupid, maybe ill-willed, but this type of information is multiplying.

The explanation could be the people's temptation to be attracted to the sensational. This kind of behavior must necessarily be linked to bad deeds, as he sees on TV, where many thefts, murders, and rapes seem to be more attractive than rewarding valuable children, for example.

Let's just think about the fact that we all received almost every day dubious messages on different communication channels. Some of us realize it's a lie, others don't.

So many people blindly listen, almost literally, to subliminal urges to distribute, such as SHARE NOW!

FAKE NEWS IS HERE TO STAY!

Those who put another new brick in the wall between truth and manipulation, which we could call *the Great Wall of Conspiracies*, know how to sell such a product. Everything is according to the successful model CALL NOW! CALL NOW!

As that harmless model of selling is working every time, we have always lived and we will continue to live with fake news from now on.

We have no way of knowing, but it could merely be the aura of secrecy that surrounds it. More than this, it could be simply our world, a world in which traditional values lose ground to this madness called '*TV rating*'.

We first encountered fake news in the Roman Empire. Since then, more information was available, and since then, we still have such theories.

They come and go, but new ones always appear each day, because there is a genuine attraction for people who try to make sense of events that are far beyond their control.

After all, who knows what is going on in that world of people somewhere above us?

All the more for those who have the exercise of the world of politics, where the truth could be of many kinds, but rarely or not at all exposed to those below.

The sad part would be that, no matter how hard we try to research, to look for scientific solutions, we cannot find them.

We will only come to the unhappy conclusion that conspiracy theories are a permanent part of the human condition.

Who Rules the World?

It has always tempted those who know almost nothing about Feemansory to believe that Freemasonry rules the world.

They have the impression that they would know what is going on inside Freemasonry, beyond the Gates of the Temple. Of course, if they would at least know what that means.

When I was at the beginning of this road, I neither knew nor was interested in this aspect, because I belong to that category of people interested in *Spirit*, not *Matter*.

These people rejoice when they can help others or when they can respond to a simple request for help, and do not rejoice when others are sick or they're in trouble.

In other words, we are talking here about that category of people who think of others, too, not only of themselves and, at most, of their family and relatives…

Now, after so many years since I set out on my Path of improvement, I could say that I already think I might know.

---

*No, Freemasonry does not rule
the world, so it seems. Those very
rich can rule the world, or, maybe,
who knows what convergent or
divergent groups of theirs,
maybe the Jesuits.*

*It could be whichever you believe,
not necessarily the Masons…*

THINGS TO REMEMBER

Therefore, the author assumes no responsibility for any misinterpretations by the uninitiated ones.

I believe that openness to the profane world, the world of the uninitiated, that is, must exist.

The Internet is a miracle nowadays, it is not something that has always existed.

Not everyone can understand the dangers of false or falsified information.

After all, who knows what is going on in that world of people somewhere above?

No, Freemasonry does not rule the world, so it seems. Those very rich can rule the world, or, maybe, who knows what convergent or divergent groups of theirs, maybe the Jesuits.

It could be whichever you believe, not necessarily the Masons...

THE LIGHT WITHIN YOU

Just a Bunch of Little Boys

Some say that many of us act like children all of our life, and that is commendable. Not always and not everywhere...

*Is that why there are so many
Masonic Organizations,
and no Light at all?*

If you pay a little more attention to the so-called social life, I mean the one on *Facebook*, *Twitter*, or *Instagram*, for example, what would you notice?

You will see many so-called Masons who prove to you that this is exactly what they wanted, and this is exactly what they have!

And, because they paid for it, they overwhelm us with images where they brag, like some far too childish kindergarten children, with their Masonic insignia.

Moreover, you can see some of them posing in Regalia, if they somehow would understand what that means, through who knows what miracle, and they expose themselves publicly as if they had won the First Prize in primary school!

*Is that what you would like to
find in Freemasonry nowadays,
to end up like these
little boys with little ambition?*

Maybe not. But, also, the answer could be YES, because that's all some of us want!

Alright, but where is the Light that the Masons are looking for?

Well, it might be at the bottom of a pit!

What's beyond it?

NOTHING.

Just the reflected image of the one looking down. So much, nothing more!

Normally, any pit is just a dead-end without a trace of Light at its end...

If you don't already have the Light in you, no matter how small, even a spark of Light, like hope, you have nothing to find down there.

The Light is Within you or Not at All!

It all seems to depend on education...

It's about what your parents taught you first, at home.

Then, comes the school.

Then, what you learn after graduation.

I have to point out that there are exceptions here, but a few rotten apples can ruin all the others!

If most are, as I should say, less educated, starting at home, and less smart, but decide that everything you need to know, you can learn on the street, not at school, this is the way it will be, in the end!

Among all these fools, the fool is you, not them, because they will overwhelm you, being too many.

If you do not have the Light in you, you will, of course, be able to walk through the darkness, but it will always strike you.

This does not mean that fate is against you or that life is terrible for you.

No one is guilty when:

- *you do not know;*
- *you have not read;*
- *you have not learned;*
- *your culture, equal to zero, does not defend you.*

EDUCATION IS YOUR SALVATION!

But what should matter to a Mason, if not a cultural base, at least? We can't exaggerate now and get people to read books by force, can we?

After all, no one forced you to become a Mason.

I've been there before, not once, but many times. I'm wondering if I might want to join nowadays such a group of people who boast that they have somehow joined this organization called Freemasonry.

Maybe I'm exaggerating, being myself an exaggerated Puritan, with a boundless lack of understanding, as some would think.

And, then, why should we lower the standards set over 300 years ago?

Just to make the number of contributions higher?

Just for the money?

Why should we lower the standards when entering Freemasonry? Just to get as many as possible to pay?

Follow the Money!

Why would anyone want to have in his yard as many Masons as possible?

Well, who would want to have more members in any kind of association, just to have some dues?

The contributions/dues matter!

For those who still remember something from elementary math, it's simple.

*The more people who pay a fee,
the higher it is, how do we call it,
just to sound better?*

No matter how much we try to avoid this extremely important issue of *contributions/dues*, as well as the number of those who pay it, this is nothing more than *benefit/profit*!

*Whose benefit is to have as many
members as possible,
not to call it profit?*

Of the giver or the receiver?

Not all the Gates Lead to the Light

Some Gates lead to nowhere...

Well, this is a complicated issue and, despite appearances, it is not specific to any geographical area.

That's why we'll treat it in more detail later because it's worth knowing which door you tap on, isn't it?

For there are enough gates, thank God!

Some are more spectacularly and attractively colored than others, to confuse and deceive the Profane who seeks the Light behind them.

Remember that not all the Gates
lead to the Light.
Some will take you nowhere...

'It may be insinuated that Freemasonry degenerates and that it loses every day the love of the good Masons and the esteem of the profane, by the ease with which the Masonic initiation is granted to all.

This remark, though repeated in every way, without reflection and to the point of satiety, is not to be disdained, and I will answer it.

We do receive, with some lightness, individuals unworthy of being admitted into a body as distinguished as that of the Freemasons: but what can we conclude from this?

That the whole association is corrupt, because some of its members are not blameless?'[1]

---

[1] *" On insinuera peut-être que la Franche-Maçonnerie dégénère et qu'elle perd chaque jour l'amour des bons Maçons et l'estime des profanes, par la facilité que l'on met à accorder à tout le monde l'initiation maçonnique.*
Cette remarque, quoique répétée à tout propos, sans réflexion et jusqu'à satiété, n'est point à dédaigner, et je vais y répondre.

This is a quote from a book published hundreds of years ago. The author is a Frenchman, *E. E. Bazot.*

There is not much to comment on here. We could easily escape by saying that it has always been like that, that, look, over 200 years ago, there were about the same problems, that we are human beings, and so on...

So be it, at first sight...

At a second glance, you would sit and wonder how many such *'organisms as distinguished as the Masons'* can exist in one country!

And then, it's quite normal to ask yourself:

---

*Is it worth it to want to be a
Mason today?*

It might be difficult to find out what an objective answer could be. More than this, it would be a tough question because of the sincerity it involves on both sides: the one who asks, but also the one who would try to answer.

All the less, it could be easy to say just as simple:

Yes or no!

Let's see why...

On reçoit effectivement, avec quelque légèreté, des individus peu dignes d'être admis dans un corps aussi distingué que est celui des Francs-Maçons: mais que conclure de là?
Que l'association entière est corrompue, parce que quelques-uns de ses membres ne sont pas irréprochables?"
Bazot, E. E., *Manuel du Franc-Maçon*, J. Moronval, Paris, 1817, p. 13

I would like to say just a few more generous words at the end of what I have said so far.

This is what I wrote in my book *'Freemasonry, my discreet life,'* and I'm also trying to emphasize whenever I have the opportunity:

*All I'm waiting for is to see
more Freemasonry in people,
not more people in Freemasonry!*

THINGS TO REMEMBER

Is that why there are so many Masonic Organizations and no Light at all?

Is that what you would like to find in Freemasonry nowadays, to end up like these little boys with little ambition?

If you don't already have the Light in you, no matter how small, even a spark of Light, like hope, you have nothing to find down there.

I have to point out that there are exceptions here, but a few rotten apples can ruin all the others!

Among all these fools, the fool is you, not them, because they will overwhelm you, being too many.

After all, no one forced you to become a Mason!

Why should we lower the standards
when entering Freemasonry?
Just to get as many as possible to pay?

The more people who pay a fee, the higher it is, how do we call it, just to sound better?

Whose benefit is to have as many members as possible, not to call it profit?

Of the giver or the receiver?

**Remember that not all the Gates lead to the Light.
Some will take you nowhere...**

Is it worth it to want to be a Mason today?

All I'm waiting for is to see more Freemasonry in people, not more people in Freemasonry!

THE VALUE OF A MASON

What Could Freemasonry Teach Us?

We are not all the same. Therefore, as human beings, Masons are not all the same. So it should not surprise us that the impact of the Masonic Teachings differs from Brother to Brother.

Therefore, I used *'what Freemasonry could teach us'* instead of a definite *'what Freemasonry teaches us.'*

In the beginning, I wasn't able to answer such a question. Now, after almost 30 years, the situation might look different.

> *I could say that I know now what Freemasonry taught me: the dignity of being a Mason.*

We may ask if others could say something like that. Did Freemasonry have the same effect on them?

These words might sound a little exaggerated to many of us, perhaps even false and bombastic.

They might be the ones who didn't understand at first and still don't understand what it means to be a Mason.

On the other hand, it might be like they didn't even suspect it before becoming Masons. Maybe I didn't imagine either.

> *Their problem is that they did not understand what it means to be a Mason even after the Initiation.*
>
> *Neither immediately, nor later...*

We are talking about those who came to the Craft for various reasons not at all related to their spiritual evolution, nor to the old and generous ideals of Freemasonry.

Unfortunately, the number of these Brethren is growing. Their percentage is worrying.

Some might say that this might be, after all, nothing more than my perception. In other words, it could be the effect on my evolution after so many years from my Initiation.

Therefore, everything could be a matter of different perceptions, subjective ones, in any case.

On the other hand, some others might say that times have changed, and I have become, let's put it this way, too the '*Worshipful.*'

Moreover, I could no longer understand the '*Zeitgeist.*'[1]

Here I think I have the right answer:

The world did not begin with me,
and perhaps even less with them,

----

[1] The defining spirit or mood of a particular period of history as shown by the ideas and beliefs of the time. Recorded from the mid 19th century, the word is German, and comes from Zeit 'time' + Geist 'spirit'.
Oxford Reference
https://www.oxfordreference.com/search?q=ZEITGEIST&searchBt n=Search&isQuickSearch=true

who did not live
so long in a Masonic spirit.

I cannot condemn someone who's trying and trying repeatedly, but, unfortunately, cannot rise to the much higher demand of an organization like Freemasonry.

Likewise, I believe that there are some goals that any of us could try to achieve by successive attempts to overcome our condition.

Of course, this is possible only if he can overcome the limitations produced by the environment in which he lives. The limitations are those produced by his world.

And here, to be able to discuss notions that must be clear to all of us, I think we need to talk about *human dignity* in general.

Thus, we could understand what would be the minimum requirements for a man to have the qualities required by Masonic Initiation.

So, what kind of man should be a true Mason?

I will try to be more explicit using some ideas that I presented in full in another book of mine: '*Freemasonry, my discreet life.*'

What is Dignity?

Count Pico della Mirandola[2] published in 1486 his famous *'Oration on the Dignity of Man'* (*Oratio de dignitate hominis*). This famous book speaks, among other things, about free will. Only man has the opportunity to choose his path in life.

'Human dignity is the result of human activity' are the words of Count Pico della Mirandola.

> „God the Father, the Mightest Architect, [...] the Divine Artificer still longed for some creature which might comprehend the meaning of so vast an achievement, which might be moved with love at its beauty and smitten with awe at its grandeur. [...]
>
> Taking man, therefore, this creature of an indeterminate image, He set him in the middle of the world and thus spoke to him: [...] you, by contrast, impeded by no such restrictions, may, by your own free will, to whose custody We have assigned you, trace for yourself the lineaments of your nature.
>
> [...] We have made you a creature neither of heaven nor earth, neither mortal nor immortal, so that you may, as the free and proud shaper of your being, fashion yourself in the form you may prefer.

---

[2] Giovanni Pico della Mirandola (1463–94), an Italian humanist and philosopher, spent part of his life at Florence in the circle of Lorenzo de' Medici. Oxford Reference https://www.oxfordreference.com/search?q=Pico+della+Mirandola+&searchBtn=Search&isQuickSearch=true

> **It will be in your power to descend to the lower, brutish forms of life; you will be able, through your own decision, to rise again to the superior orders whose life is divine.'[3]**

Nowadays, looking in the *Merriam–Webster* dictionary for an updated meaning of *human dignity*, we would find this definition:

> **The quality of being worthy of honor or respect; formal reserve or seriousness of manner, appearance, or language; the quality or state of being worthy, honored, or esteemed.[4]**

This is what we accept today, not when *Pico della Mirandola* lived.

Unfortunately, people and, of course, Masons, would mean by this term only a sort of simple social position, so to speak, as a political position somewhere in the Government would be.

Even in our newest dictionaries, there is more talk about this than about dignity as a *human quality*.

We could say that those who see in dignity only a social and political position, no matter how important might be, are those who illustrate a characteristic of dignity: that of being the barometer of a man's price.

---

[3] Giovanni Pico della Mirandola, ORATION ON THE DIGNITY OF MAN, 1486

[4] Merriam-Webster https://www.merriam-webster.com/dictionary/dignity

Every man has his price.

Depending on how many compromises and concessions someone has made during his own life, and how many debts they have accumulated, and I mean here moral debts, especially, that man is more or less for sale.

So, in a world where almost all people are for sale, only the price is different.

That's all...

Are we Really Impostors, all of Us?

The dignity of the profane life, that high social or political position, may very well be because of the party you are in, your relatives, or your relationships.

No sign here of any real merit.

On the other hand, we might say that any parent may believe that his child is the smartest and most beautiful child in the world.

This is a natural thing, which is understandable, after all, and there is nothing wrong with that.

Thus, the parent feels that his child should have more than his father, for instance, because he wants more for his child.

So, if given the opportunity, the child who has now become a mature man will always be promoted higher and faster than others.

Their misfortune would be just the fact that they don't have the chance of having some better '*connected*' relatives.

Nothing more...

We might forgive a parent for promoting non-values, up to a point, but why would Masons lower the standards of Freemasonry?

Promoting Non-Values

Let's just think a while about this:

Who is our biggest enemy, if not us, through lack of will and just an arrogant desire for power?

Now, let's see...

If we look in the mirror, what will we see?

Don't we see in the mirror exactly our enemy, the one who stops us from progressing on our Path?

As human beings, so many of us are, unfortunately, nothing more than selfish impostors...

Almost all of us could be bigger or smaller impostors.
How small or how big, this is something that it really doesn't matter!

The problem is that, sincerely or not, we believe we are more than we could ever be.

Of course, we could say that this characteristic is in our human beings and we have nothing to do.

But, watch out, could this excuse be enough to get us out of any guilt?

After all, Masons are people too...

I'm not the one to judge, or to give solutions.

I just dare to ask.

The entry into the Masonic Order of some people promoted politically, which falls into the realm of political clientelism, is of no use to anyone.

And, because of this subtle infiltration, the quality of the members of the Order could decrease constantly, day by day...

By the deeds of these uninvited Brethren, the other Masons, who have come to the Temple with a pure heart and in good faith to seek the Light, are also soiled, without being guilty.

A worthy Mason is the mirror of Freemasonry.

Every day, we notice how ideas like *dignity* or *honor* become things that have no value anymore in a society with revolting values.

In order not to get lost on your Masonic Path, you must remain dignified in your actions and hope that others will appreciate that.

If we want to be completely free men, who cannot be bought, we should first learn to behave in a dignified way in the profane life.

THINGS TO REMEMBER

I could say that I know now what Freemasonry taught me: the dignity of being a Mason.

Their problem is that they did not understand what means to be a Mason even after the Initiation. Neither immediately nor later...

The world did not begin with me, and perhaps even less with them, who did not live so long in a Masonic spirit.

Every man has his price.

We might forgive a parent for promoting non-values, up to a point, but why would Masons lower the standards of Freemasonry?

Who is our biggest enemy if not us, through lack of will but an arrogant desire for power?

We could almost all of us be bigger or smaller impostors.
How small or how big, this is something that it really doesn't matter!

After all, Masons are people too...
I'm not here the one to judge, nor to give solutions.
I just dare to ask.

A worthy Mason is the mirror of Freemasonry.

If we want to be completely free men, who cannot be bought, we should, first, learn to behave in a dignified way in the profane life.

THE BIGGEST CHANGE

That Small Change in You

All those who came to understand know that the great culprit for what they are doing wrong is not outside of them. The problem is themselves.

And may want to change, but...

How should they change?

What else can someone rely on today?

A New World, but the same People?

Look, it's been a while since the end of the world, the year 2000, I presume.

Anyhow, this would be the last Apocalypse we've missed.

For those who didn't even notice, we, the people, Masons or not, have remained the same. Or so it seems to us…

After all, we are all human beings, not *ET*s. So, it could be hard to see yourself as you are.

On the other hand, it could be much easier to see the faults of others, unfortunately.

Therefore, the mistakes made by some Lodges or Grand Lodges are very obvious to me.

Having so many years of Freemasonry behind me, I can't help it.

I simply notice them, even if I've been wearing glasses for some time.

Maybe I look like one of the two old men in the *Muppets*, nice people, I'd say, you know, those two who always had something to say.

And what they were criticizing could be very entertaining.

By contrast, what I have to say might not be funny at all.

Everything has an explanation, but…

The most important thing would be this:

> *Let's not forget that Freemasonry comprises people who are subject to passions and mistakes.*

We are talking here about values that have proved their validity for thousands and thousands of years, and now they suddenly are beginning to tremble.

And yet they have been the basis of the great religions that have morally shaped humanity for thousands of years.

Unfortunately, the expansion of the Internet is no stranger to this unfortunate phenomenon.

New Worlds in Collision

Moral certainties are now considered worthy of questioning by people who do not even know what they are talking about and, more than that, people who may not even know what they want.

These circumstantial revolutionaries live in a world that is extremely limited by their lack of education, not to mention anything about their lack of an overview.

> *We live in a world where old values are literally torn down from their foundations.*

Some minorities, more or less important in size, are beginning to raise their voices and impose their dictates, while the majority is giving in more and more, step by step.

This strange process probably takes place out of an excessive delicacy bordering on stupidity and unconsciousness.

Scientists already predict that the Great End is not far off, so nothing else matters?

Does it matter, then, the impotence of the majority in the face of a bunch of minorities guided, paid, and led from behind the front?

'*Which front?*', you may ask.

Who leads from a distance, not only subliminally, these not too educated people who want, in their unconsciousness, to burn the very earth on which they live?

Cui Prodest?

What do you mean, we've already forgotten Latin, right now, when it's already banned from some universities?

'*Cui prodest?*'

In plain English: '*Who benefits?*'

It's quite simple, you just have to see WHO MIGHT USE the destruction of our civilization, the Western Civilization.

The result is that this impotence of the majority sells the future of mankind as if the world would end with it.

Maybe that's indeed the case.

The world may even end because of the unconsciousness of these minorities of all kinds.

THINGS TO REMEMBER

The result is that this impotence of the majority sells the future of mankind as if the world would end with it. Maybe that's the case.

Let's not forget that Freemasonry comprises people who are subject to passions and mistakes.

We live in a world where old values are literally torn down from their foundations.

Scientists already predict that the Great End is not far off, so nothing else matters?

THE NEW INQUISITION

Unconsciousness Could Kill?

So it seems that this impotence of the majority could sell our future.

Could this mean Apocalypse Now?

Let's be even clearer than this...

The world could end because
of the irresponsibility
of minorities of all kinds.

And, look, the individualism and petty interests of small groups are slowly entering and altering all areas of our lives, as they have been so far.

The pillars on which human
society should be based:
Family,
Church,
Community
and the Fatherland
are attacked from several sides.

The new Human Character

What can better shape the human character nowadays?

Television?

The Internet?

At first glance, TV is the biggest culprit for changing the value system valid for so many thousands of years.

It's also easy to be fooled by the seemingly inexhaustible supply of information.

More than that, it may be hard to understand. How can you believe that the more information there is, the harder it is for you to choose what is true and what is less true?

Even harder it will be to see what is pure manipulation. Apparently, you have at your disposal those countless channels that seem to be the most objective source for you.

Apparently…

To all this nonsense we must add, perhaps, the almighty Internet with that unfortunate access that is far too open. The problem is that this allows any individual, regardless of their level of education, to give lessons to others anywhere on Earth.

Let's try to explain this, though…

A new Inquisition?

Far be it from me the idea of imprisonment in the past of the Inquisition, for example, right now, when a kind of totally new re-democratization process is on the rise.

*Do you have to be a Mason
if you want to heal
this sick world we live in?*

You need to understand more than what they taught you. Here, *'taught'* is synonymous with *'manipulate.'*

Even this reminds me of Orwell, I wish that, this time at least, I could be wrong.

Then, you might notice that a certain openness to the lower strata of society has its subtle pitfalls.

Everything is just like any other well-orchestrated *'political campaign.'*

*The speculations of anyone who
comes to the pulpit have replaced
the wise sermon of the priest.*

*The most visible are of those who
have nothing good to share and
would rather be silent.*

COMMAND+Z&CTRL+Z, Anytime, Anywhere?

It would be good if you could only have access to what is good and true.

Yes, unfortunately, the people who you should listen to know their limits.

*"I know that I know nothing" is
something completely unknown to
an uneducated man.*

This saying, derived from Plato's account of Socrates is, however, very well known by educated people.

They are humbler, too.

The result is that those who should be silent talk far too much and hurt others, but also them because they also believe in their nonsense.

So, you can't silence those who want evil, even their own, without realizing it. You have no choice.

Of course, you might change the website or TV channel. Apparently, it's simple and, moreover, it seems to be at your will.

Well, with some limits imposed by profile obtained from your own information and interactions (in a sort of the Secret Service style).

To numb your remaining reflexes and subliminally attract you, your profile is made by many means that have cute names, such as *'cookies,'* just to numb your reflexes...

*Have you ever thought that the
remote control is, in fact, not in
your hand, but the hands of those
controlling you?*

Anyway, anyone can say anything, anytime.

And this happens anyhow, because everyone has the right to speak, right?

And this doesn't just happen at a barbecue in the small yard behind the house, with a beer in hand, just in front of the family, but publicly on the *Almighty Internet!*

Many of these uneducated people
challenged everything,
even history, as if everything
would work
with Command / CTRL + Z!

Well, no!

That's not the way things are.

Not everything works
with CTRL + Z!

Not even with ⌘ + Z!

And that's especially true in all circumstances when you don't even know what you want, and you have nothing to rely on.

Then it would be the perfect moment for you to be silent.

But you definitely have something to say, even if you know nothing about it.

The reason would be simply your lack of education and intelligence, in the first place.

Or maybe, the explanation that you can't shut up, and you have to say something, anything, just talk, would be the simple fact that just last night you saw someone on TV.

And that one was saying that he had no idea about a certain subject. But, anyhow, he indeed had to show he wasn't too stupid, as it was, so he had to say another stupid thing:

"My opinion is that..."

Well, if the person invited to talk on television can speak without understanding the subject, why not you?

If you listen to what the educated ones have to say, you could learn something.

If you listen to what uneducated people always have to say, you'll be wasting a part of your life.

That part we call *time*.

And no one can give you time back.

THINGS TO REMEMBER

The world could end because of the irresponsibility of minorities of all kinds.

The pillars on which human society should be based: the Family, the Church, the Community, and the Fatherland are attacked from several sides.

At first glance, the TV is the biggest culprit for changing the value system valid for so many thousands of years.

Do you have to be a Mason if you want to heal this sick world we live in?

The speculations of anyone who comes to the pulpit have replaced the wise sermon of the priest.

The most visible are of those who have nothing good to share and would rather be silent.

"I know that I know nothing" is something completely unknown to an uneducated man.

Have you ever thought that the remote control is, in fact, not in your hand, but the hands of others who control you?

Most of them even challenged everything, even the history, as if everything would work with Command / CTRL + Z!

Not everything works with CTRL + Z!
Not even with ⌘ + Z!

And no one can give you time back.

THE NEW WORLD ORDER

War and Freemasonry

What could such a combination mean?

There are two explanations here. We relate the first one to the fight against Freemasonry. The second is about the New World Order.

Let's look at what the ANTI-MASONIC MOVEMENT would be and how much is this related to the truth.

Some over 200 years ago, John Robison[1] published a book called *'Proofs of a Conspiracy against all the Religions and Governments of Europe, carried on in the Secret Meetings of Free-Masons, Illuminati and Reading Societies, etc., collected from good authorities'*, published in 1797.

The title of this book could be the first sign that reveals the reactionary character of the one who references France in the book, immediately after the Revolution of 1792.

Not to mention that apparently, it condemns reading, because it also refers to Reading Societies as a very evil thing!!!

Finally...

Being British, he loves France madly, especially a republican one, doesn't he?

And then he becomes a really bad boy...

He does not necessarily attack Freemasonry in his book, but the influence of a certain secret society. Robison, right from the introduction, refers to the unfortunate influence of the Bavarian *Illuminati* society.

---

[1] **British physicist and mathematician, member of the Edinburgh Philosophical Society**

Robison's ideas caught on to the public, drawn to mysteries, and this word, Illuminati, means a lot even nowadays.

Illuminati, Masons, and Jesuits

John Robison was trying to prove that there has to be a causal link between the Bavarian Illuminati, French Freemasonry, and, of course, the French Revolution.

Almost everything written in his book was nothing more than misleading information. Or rather, lies that catch on with the public.

With the beginning of the twentieth century, new theories appeared, also because of the success enjoyed by those of Marx.

A controversial author, Nesta Helen Webster is successful in spreading a mixture of conspiracy theories, some fresh blood for the people.

Anyone could now find that almost everything that is somehow mysterious, apparently comes from the Illuminati.

And behold, this woman has an even richer imagination, because she gathers together Masons, Jesuits, the Hebrew Kabbalah, the French Revolution, the 1848 Revolution, and Lenin's Bolshevik Revolution, etc.

The result is some pure anti-Semitism and, of course, the anti-Masonic current.

Together, they would form what we call now *the Judeo-Masonic conspiracy.*

The idea of a Judeo-Masonic conspiracy would later be a term cherished by all fascist and Nazi movements until the end of World War II.

Today, with the help of the Internet, these theories are spreading even easier, unfortunately...

Sometimes you don't have to be the change. It can be a big event, like a war.

This is exactly what happened after the Second World War because the First World War brought us the disintegration of those big empires, but also Communism...

The New World Order

Generally, the transition to the *New World Order*, the *Cold War*, the clash of civilizations in *Huntington*'s theories, as we want to call it, meant not only the division of the world into *Capitalism* and *Communism*.

*The madness and unconsciousness
after the First World War
inevitably led to the Crisis of
1929.*

It couldn't have ended any other way, with those crazy years after 1920, that period called 'Les *années folles*,' we would say now.

Who said the winds of change were already blowing.

Mussolini and *Hitler* only had to seize that historic moment.

*You don't have to be a Mason to
understand all this, but it would
have been great if the Masons
could have done something then.*

When Freemasonry could intervene, already banned by Hitler or Stalin wherever they could, it was too late.

The Hollywood Mistake

The sweetened silence of the propaganda imposed by the *Hollywood* movies ended up giving an inverse reaction, of repulsion towards a distorted reality.

Hollywood-type reality meant some elegant men dressed at any hour of the day or night as if they were going to a wedding right then. Women were floating diaphanously in settings that curled the reality of people who lived normally.

It was like a sort of continuous prom setting, and this had determined, after all, the revolt against the System.

There was a need for a new religion, the religion of a truly new world.

Neither millennial Christianity nor secular Humanism kept up with the times.

The idea of the Church is no longer '*cool*,' this is already obvious. Not to mention the *Notre Dame* flames, which send another message.

But this is quite another very long story, related to the end of European civilization and could not be the subject of this book, which refers to Freemasonry.

More than this, it may not be quite a *politically correct* subject, God forbid!

Only Freemasonry has maintained its values and reputation with no stain.

The loss of interest in the Church, as a respectable and necessary institution, is a longer process, which probably began around the end of World War II.

New Age, the New Temple

Any rope stretched too much, breaks, in the end, that much is clear.

Therefore, the people of the 1950s, especially the new generations, did not swallow all the lies of the System so easily.

As a result, they replaced the far too impeccable *Cary Grant* with the much more human and, tragically for him, the one with hesitant sexuality, although he seemed to be quite a real man: *James Dean.*

Likewise, slowly, going through the *Flower Power Movement,* so many people, or at least some of them, in the beginning, replaced the old Church and its Christian morality with the seemingly more human teachings of Buddhism.

They perfectly summed their way of thinking in their famous slogan:

MAKE LOVE, NOT WAR!

Probably, those people were considering these teachings different and far more interesting. More than that, those teachings of Buddhism were new for them, and, perhaps, full of wisdom and goodness.

All this time, Freemasonry has continued to maintain its reputation as a solid rock that withstands the gusts of water.

And this is how the *New Age Movement* appears, which is a completely different way from any other form of official religion.

With no Vatican of its own, the New Age Movement is a kind of spiritual movement springing from enthusiasm.

Stadiums took the place of churches as a place of 'gathering'. This new generation in jeans no longer felt at ease in the somehow oppressive space of a church, even if it was an enormous cathedral.

Young people, in the seventh decade of the twentieth century, felt the need to come together in much larger communities, much like in *Woodstock*.

If the church was no longer
a suitable place,
how would he fit in here
The Masonic Temple?

THINGS TO REMEMBER

Robison's ideas caught on to the public, drawn to mysteries, and this word, Illuminati, means a lot even nowadays.

A controversial author, Nesta Helen Webster is indeed successful in spreading a mixture of conspiracy theories, some fresh blood for the people.

The idea of a Judeo-Masonic conspiracy will be later a term cherished by all the fascist and Nazi movements until the end of World War II.

Sometimes you don't have to be the change. It can be a big event, like a war.

The madness and unconsciousness after the First World War inevitably led to the Crisis of 1929.

You don't have to be a Mason to understand all this, but it would have been great if the Masons could have done something then.

Neither millennial Christianity nor secular Humanism managed to keep up with the times.

Only Freemasonry has maintained its values and reputation without any stain.

MAKE LOVE, NOT WAR!

All this time, Freemasonry has continued to maintain its reputation, as a solid rock that withstands the gusts of water.

With no Vatican of its own, the New Age Movement is a kind of spiritual movement springing from enthusiasm.

If the church was no longer a suitable place, how would he fit in here, in The Masonic Temple?

IS FREEMASONRY RIGHT FOR YOU?

Freemasonry from Inside You

hen you look at the bottom of a fountain, you see nothing but yourself and your world. No matter how much you try to see further, you will only find the answers to your questions inside you.

Only when you find the answer will Masonry appear. If it shows up, of course.

This will happen exactly when you are ready to see more, exactly when the time for it has come.

Everything happens only if you can seize the moment. If the assault of information from the material world, the one where we all live, already overwhelmed you, you could miss this moment.

Freemasonry could help you find your special place in a world that no longer seems to be yours. Usually, your world was always changing and seemed to forget about yourself almost all the time.

> *Freemasonry could be an oasis of peace in a desert where storms sweep everything.*

Now, it might be true that not everybody has a place in this oasis.

Maybe you don't either.

Or, you know what? Maybe this kind of peaceful place is not for you, because you think you are, or probably you indeed are, a sort of rebel disturbed by any kind of peace.

Maybe any moral code, like any law that protects the weak from the one who is too strong, is not for you.

You might believe that such a code is, in principle, something that you should avoid or even violate, because, otherwise, you would feel like an ordinary man.

If you think you are smart and the others are just some fools, let them enter Freemasonry!

Surely, Freemasonry is not for you!

From time immemorial, Freemasonry has been like a kind of guiding beacon for those on ships in distress.

It did not feel threatened by the large gatherings, for it was never more than a gathering place for a smaller group of people.

When you need it, then Freemasonry is right inside you!

Freemasonry Today

How can Freemasonry fit as a discreet organization in the picture so complex and difficult to understand in today's world?

*Why it would be worth it to be a
Mason just nowadays when
everything seems
to be different from when
Freemasonry appeared,
over 300 years ago?*

We can only find the answer to these questions if we understand well or, more precisely, if we understand the essence of being a Mason.

More than that...

You should understand what Freemasonry existed before and after the crossroads of 1717, what were the ideals that brought about change in those times, such as the Masons at the time, etc.

Let's try to find an answer or at least some options that can be shown to us in the Path we choose to follow...

*However, we must not forget
that the answer
is always somewhere inside us.*

All we have to do is look for it!

What is Freemasonry?

In the beginning, the Masons were the builders of cathedrals.

That's right...

They formed a kind of guild with special privileges.

That's right too...

On the other hand, they were not noble, even if they had some privileges. Therefore, they were in high demand. Masons were free people who could travel anywhere. The rest of the people were not so lucky.

The time came for the changes brought by the Renaissance, so the stonemasons' guild admitted members who were no longer operative, i.e. masons or stonemasons.

A group of people who had not laid hands on a chisel in their lives, nor had they worked in building cathedrals, as the ancient Masons had done, gathered to build something else.

They wanted to build what they wanted to be an *Ideal Temple of Humanity*.

That was the magic moment in time: London, 1717.

> **One of the oldest social and charitable organizations in the world, Freemasonry's roots lie in the traditions of the medieval stonemasons who built our cathedrals and castles.**

> **For Freemasons, there are four important values that help define their path through life: Integrity, Friendship, Respect, and Charity.**
>
> **In today's world filled with uncertainty, these principles ring as true now as they have at any point in the organization's history.**[1]

As it says here, the most respected Masonic body in the world, i.e. UGLE, the principles of Freemasonry are the same from all times, valid then and now.

Are You a Freemason?

If we were to speak in very fashionable terms nowadays, Freemasonry seems to be recommended to those who feel alone, do not have many friends, live a social life at most online.

There is no limitation or discrimination here, as is fashionable now, God forbid. And this recommendation is valid only if those who knock at the Gate want to study the philosophy behind Masonic Teachings.

---

[1] UGLE, About Freemasonry, https://www.ugle.org.uk/about-freemasonry

*If you feel you resonate
with Masonic ideals, you can
knock stress-free at the Gate!*

The one who understands that Freemasonry is not any kind of secret society, the place for all sorts of conspiracies, more and more spectacular, is on the right track.

It would be even better if understand that all these things catch the best to the public, and Freemasonry is but an organization that tries, at least, to make better people.

Anyone who doesn't understand this should think about *Google, Apple, Microsoft,* or *Shell* management meetings, for example.

Are they public, somehow?

Why would anyone who doesn't have shares in these big names be interested in what is being discussed there?

Well, aren't they public or not?

That means they have something to hide.

They want to establish a dictatorship, right?

Well, fairy tales could be delightful, but at their time, when we talk with children, not mature people, even if they have no head to judge at all.

Some may see in the Teachings of Freemasonry a kind of personality development program, something that has been in vogue for some time.

Others will find a place where you can meet people from whom you can learn, people who welcome you with open arms, without the reluctance of life beyond the Temple.

In the Lodge, you feel at home among the Brethren, and that matters, perhaps, the most.

It's hard to see this when you're not among them, unfortunately.

Hence, so many assumptions and conspiracy theories that do not do good to Freemasonry, but cannot affect it, being a perfect human construction, if there can be such a thing to be created by man.

Does Language Scare You?

It is not at all easy to resonate with a language used over 300 years ago in England! Just think of the language used by the old chroniclers, and you will understand the difficulty.

Originally, language seems obsolete, far too different from contemporary. It is natural to be so, for they are words from the first years of the eighteenth century, from the time of the first official documents of the United Grand Lodge of England.

The words used in the Ritual, in particular, may have a meaning that is not very similar to our language today.

This does not detract from the charm of the phrases, which sound very poetic.

If you understand you are using the same words that other Brethren have spoken so many times before you, you will feel connected to a strong tradition that has not been changed for centuries.

You walk today on the same Path followed by all the Brethren before you.

The Masonic Faith

1. There is only one God (Supreme Being), the Father of all people.

2. The Holy Bible, or Book of the Holy Law, is the Great Light in Freemasonry and is the Law and Guide in our faith and practice.

3. The soul is immortal.

4. Character determines destiny.

5. Love of God is man's first duty.

6. Man's love is man's second duty.

7. The truth is good.

8. Communion with God in the form of prayer brings much good.

Masonic Teachings

It may be impossible to make a summary of the Masonic Teachings.

Let us try, however, so that we can understand regardless of whether we have reached the necessary level of spiritual development...

Freemasonry teaches us:

- to practice mercy and goodwill;

- to protect chastity;

- to respect the ties of blood and friendship;

- to adopt the principles and to respect the religious precepts;

- to help the weak;

- to guide the blind man;

- to raise the fallen;

- to help the orphan;

- to guard the Altar;

- to support those who lead the country;

- to inspire morality;

- to promote learning;
- to love people;
- to respect God and ask for His mercy;
- to hope for happiness.

THINGS TO REMEMBER

Freemasonry could be an oasis of peace in a desert where storms sweep everything.

If you think you are smart and the others are just some fools, let them enter Freemasonry!

Surely, Freemasonry is not for you!

When you need it, then Freemasonry is right inside you!

Why it would be worth it to be a Mason just today, when everything seems to be different than when Freemasonry appeared, over 300 years ago?

However, we must not forget that the answer is always somewhere inside us.

All we have to do is look for him!

If you feel you resonate with Masonic ideals, you can knock stress-free at the Gate!

In the Lodge, you feel at home among the Brethren, and that matters, perhaps, the most.

The words used in the Ritual, in particular, may have a meaning that is not very similar to our language today.

You walk today on the same Path followed by all the Brethren before you.

FROM ONE WORLD TO ANOTHER

The Origins of the New Freemasonry

All those who laid the foundations of the new Freemasonry in 1717 were no longer workers who had gathered in a guild of cathedral builders, but nobles who admired their ideas, that is, Freemasonry.

They were accustomed to the minuet and the *Music of the Waters*, by composer *Georg Friedrich Händel*, which premiered in London in 1717, and carried the ideas of masons further into the new post-world.

Just as the world of stone craftsmen became that of nobles, the *Operative Lodges* became those of the *Accepted Masons*, that is, of those accepted as builders of cathedrals, although they were not.

Hence the acronym commonly found in Regular Lodges, that *A∴F∴&F∴M∴, (Ancient Free & Accepted Masonry)*.

By the way, very briefly now, because we will talk more about this later, the Regular Lodges are those recognized by the founders of Freemasonry in 1717, i.e., by *UGLE (United Grand Lodge of England)*.

Of course, there have been many changes in society, not to mention people, as a result of which we tend to think that the ideals of 300 years ago could differ dramatically from those of today.

*Freemasonry does not change
as society does
more and more often,
but it adapts as best it can…*

On St. John's Day, June 24, 1717, four London Lodges,
which existed for some time, met at Goose and Gridiron
Ale-house in St. Paul's Churchyard and declared the
Grand Lodge.
Anthony Sayer was elected Grand Master.
This was the first Grand Lodge of the new Freemasonry.

(https://www.ugle.org.uk/about-freemasonry/history-of-
freemasonry)

Noble or Gentleman?

The construction of cathedrals lasted several centuries, giving masons enough time to strengthen their position in society, but not enough to be considered nobles.

Those who also wanted to be part of the *Operative Lodges* were nobles with family trees of hundreds of years, and also those who formed the new nobility. People called them in French 'gentilhomme' and in English 'gentleman'.

This was a title that had a noble character, taking advantage of this moment at the beginning of the eighteenth century.

There were no more grandiose works to be done, so the Operative Lodges began to receive new members, who were 'accepted'.

Hence the name of the new Freemasonry. They were not truly Masons, according to the old rules in force at the Operative Lodges until then.

If we pay attention to the subtleties of the meaning of this term, at the beginning of the eighteenth century, in English or French, we will easily notice the difference. The meaning was *'gentle people'*, i.e. *'special,' 'well-educated,'* and *'of good origin.'*

It's a long way from *'gentle people'* to the plethora of smart boys presented nowadays as role models.

---

*What could a boy who knows all
the tricks look for in Freemasonry?*

I am convinced that by now, he knows the answer to any question because he already knows everything.

We will continue our search. What if we find some other explanation?

Gentleman and Millennial

Many things have changed since the time of horse-drawn carriages… We are not just talking here only about these everyday changes in technology or about the invasion of computers and increasingly smart and smarter phones, etc…

No. We are talking about us.

Are we today the same as those from the past?

Unquestionably not!

We can talk about the ease with which we communicate nowadays. We can talk about the effect of the Internet.

But we must also talk about the perhaps too rapid change of perceptions and attitudes towards problems that seemed, at other times, completely out of any discussion.

Didn't Freemasonry also become obsolete, like a horse-drawn carriage?

Can today's Freemasonry help you be different from the others?

Can Freemasonry make you a better person with no computer, mobile phone, and the Internet to complete this noble mission?

There are so many TV channels today that there seems to be no room for one dedicated to people looking for the Light.

Could the Light be beyond all these screens in which the chosen reality is mirrored, already chewed, and already digested by others for them?

Unlikely…

The Right Man, the Right Moment

We know Freemasonry does not appear in a man's life until the moment has come.

Well, it seems simple to understand that you can't become a different kind of person, a Mason, in this case, unless you realize it. But how do you know if you don't even have a call for it?

*You probably don't feel any desire
to become a Mason,
if your world is a limited one.*

Depending on what you have accumulated in the years when you should have done it, i.e., I mean until the end of your studies, whatever they may be, you could now decide which might be your unique Path.

*Your Path is unique, and this is
your Path to follow, not any other.*

Not any, but the one that is right for you or, moreover, destined for you, regardless of whether you believe that there is a destiny.

*If you think that, as some say,
the street teaches you
everything you need,
then a trickster you will become!*

Well, it's clear that then you don't even need more, maybe a Ferrari, and money, a lot of money, as much as possible.

Freemasonry is not for you, that's clear!

If you know nothing that truly matters in life, you won't be able to choose, because you don't know what to choose.

And then you stay where you are, where you like and feel good, where that Ferrari can take you, to the club, to the pub, through other such cultural centers of your level.

And that's enough for you because you don't even know you can do more than that…

And you can't because you don't know, and so on…

Another World, with the same People?

What can make you want to be a Mason these days?

Obviously, we are referring here to those who have an interest. How can we call it?

Aaaa, yes, an honest interest in becoming a member of Freemasonry!

Have you finished studying all the books you should know?

Of course, this is also a valid option if you have any ideas about what you should know.

*Maybe you don't even know that
it would be useful not only for you
to know more but also for those
who depend or will depend
on you later in life.*

Let's not exaggerate, even so, maybe you haven't even read them, or, at most, browsed?

More than that.

Free Men and Slaves

Maybe you don't even like to read, because you firmly believe that this is something outdated now when all the interesting things are there, on the digital screen.

It doesn't even have to be as big as the living room wall.

The mobile phone could also work.

Maybe this doesn't satisfy you completely either, because the screen of your mobile phone is too small compared to the big TV that you didn't buy in vain.

Not to mention that the TV is not only useful for you, but also for those who put in your head what they want.

It's not like you think you do what you want when you change the same channels on the same TV.

But you don't see that, there's no way to understand more.

You are happy that it looks good on that big screen, and here is the end of the road for you!

Why bother looking for answers to your questions on such a small screen?

Especially if, in fact, you didn't even ask a question!

If you swallow everything already prepared by others and choose from your remote what they gave you on TV, so will your life be.

A life programmed by others through your remote control.

You will be just one of those billions of remote-controlled human robots driven by others who know what they want from you!

So, sit at home, in front of your TV, and listen carefully to what you are told or, more delicate, not to be scared somehow, what they recommend you.

*If they drive you through the TV
remote control, you will not want
and will never be a Mason,
for he is a free man.*

*You're but a slave, nothing more,
and so you will remain!*

People Without God

The world is big. There's room for everyone.

Yes, except this book is about that Freemasonry founded in 1717.

Don't you like these principles?

No problem!

Grand Orient de France (GODF) is waiting for you with open arms!

Several books appeared on how the new Masons should be accepted from the beginning. The most known book is that of Anderson, from 1723.

Here is what we can read from the very beginning in what we call *Anderson's Constitutions*, regarding the most important obligation of a *Freemason Brother*, a member of the new Speculative Lodges created in 1717:

> I. Concerning GOD and RELIGION.
>
> A Mason is obliged by his Tenure, to obey the moral Law; and if he rightly understands the Art, he will never be a stupid Atheist nor an irreligious Libertine.
>
> But though in ancient Times Masons were charged in every Country to be of the Religion of that Country or Nation, whatever it was, yet 'tis now thought more expedient only to oblige them to that Religion in which all Men agree, leaving their particular Opinions to themselves;
>
> that is, to be good Men and true, or Men of Honour and Honesty, by whatever Denominations or Persuasions they may be distinguished;
>
> whereby Masonry becomes the Center of Union, and the Means of conciliating true Friendship among Persons that must have remained at a perpetual Distance.[1]

From the very beginning, we see that those who would not swear on the Bible for anything in the

---

[1] Anderson, James, The Constitutions of the Free-Masons, London, 1723

world have nothing to do with Freemasonry!

We do not care which of the evangelists of the new religion called *Personal Development* has diverted them in such a way that it has convinced them they are new gods. Of course, with a small 'g', above any teachings that have proven to be good for thousands and thousands of years.

What matters is that they take a discreet step backward and develop personally with their gods who pour the *New Education* into their heads.

They could enjoy their usual life, whatever this would be: *Facebook, Instagram,* and so on...

Wherever they are feeling good, there is their place. It could be a world without God, where they can play like some minor gods in full personal development, fighting for power.

Why would you do this?

Is there anything in human nature that turns you into a wolf? Of course, you can blame those Latins who said *Homo homini lupus est.*[2]

Is there anything in human nature that could make you hunt nothing more than money and glory?

Those who do such a thing know better, perhaps, why they worship the god of another one who wants their souls: *Money...*

---

[2] Latin proverb meaning "A man is a wolf to another man."

> *Those without God have nothing*
> *to do with Freemasonry!*

THINGS TO REMEMBER

Freemasonry does not change as society does more and more often, but it adapts as best it can...

There were no more grandiose works to be done, so the Operative Lodges began to receive new members, who are 'accepted'.

What could a boy who knows all the tricks look for in Freemasonry?

Didn't Freemasonry also become obsolete, like a horse-drawn carriage?

Freemasonry does not appear in a man's life until the moment has come.

You probably don't feel any desire to become a Mason, if your world is a limited one.

Your Path is unique and this is your Path to follow, not any other.

If you think that, as some say, the street teaches you everything you need, then a trickster you will become!

If you know nothing that truly matters in life, you won't be able to choose, because you don't know what to choose.

Maybe you don't even know that it would be
useful not only for you to know more but also
for those who depend or will depend on you
later in life.

If you swallow everything already prepared by
others and choose from your remote what they
gave you on TV, so will your life be.

A life programmed by others through your remote
control.

If you are driven from the TV remote control, you
will not want and will never be a Mason, for he
is a free man.
You're but a slave, nothing more, and so you will
remain!

From the very beginning, we see that those who
would not swear on the Bible for anything in
the world have nothing to do with
Freemasonry!

Those without God have nothing to do with
Freemasonry!

WHERE TO KNOCK AT THE DOOR?

Do all Gates Lead to the Same Place?

ecause I have many people who proudly tell me they were initiated, so we are Brethren, I know the unsuspected and always unnoticed drama of the one who did not knock on the right gate.

Well, what do you mean, you didn't knock on the right gate? Aren't all gates the same?

In an organization that has very strict rules, that does not change as the wind blows in society, in a world so well-informed today, it may not be clear where you should knock on the door?

There is only one Gate
in one organization.

At several organizations,
how could it be?

How is it possible that a confusion or, worse, a cascade of confusions, intentional or not, persists?

And this is happening despite the clear principle of exclusive territoriality, the one that recognizes only the existence of a single Grand Lodge in a country.

Everything that is not as we
would expect it to be when we
talk of a serious and respectable
organization such as Freemasonry
happens because its members are
also human beings, after all.

You indeed have no way of knowing what is beyond the Gate, when you do not have access to what is there, for reasons that are easy to understand.

All you can see outside the Gate is the sometimes excessively well-created image of those who deal with PR (Public Relations), i.e. the image of the organization in public.

In other words, it is something that has a connection with reality in a proportion that is, sometimes, not always, not to dramatize, worryingly small.

More clearly, it can be a reality slightly distorted by a lot of deformed information, which only entices and that's it.

This type of information is what you may find on the public website of a Grand Lodge, for example.

More info we will find also on the Facebook page, and in other public places, because, after entering, it is too late to regret that you did not choose another gate...

One Country, One Grand Lodge?

If we follow what those who created modern Freemasonry do, UGLE, so be it: one country = one Grand Lodge!

SO MUCH!

*The situation of the Grand
Lodges,
the situation on the ground,
not from the height of UGLE,
could be a little different...*

I do this because that's how I was taught in the Masonic Temple, that I have to help my Brother see where he went wrong.

*Just like any good Mason, I would
like to be, I always expect to be
corrected,
so I can straighten up, of course.*

Let's return to what '*territoriality*' can mean in a Masonic context ...

A very good connoisseur of the realities of this particular world, *Paul Bessel*, tells us something like this:

> **In short, decisions about which Grand Lodges to recognize should be made on the basis of which ones meet the standards established by each Grand Lodge, and not on the basis of the elusive, confusing, and often-violated doctrine of exclusive territorial jurisdiction.**

> **In fact, it might be clearer if the doctrine were simply declared to be no longer useful or in force.**[1]

Some Are good, the Others, So and So...

Now, if I want to set up a certain organization nowadays, whatever might be, and I should choose my partner organizations from other countries, of course, I would do it according to the rules established or agreed by me.

This is happening if I do not want to fall under the umbrella of a large organization, worldwide, where I do not make the rules and I have to adapt to the situation.

This is also the case with Freemasonry, where the one who decides is UGLE, which has the right, after all, as *the Grand Mother Lodge of the World*, to say who is good and who is less good, that is, regularly and irregularly.

Suppose I would like to enter Freemasonry tomorrow. What would I do after getting seriously informed on the Internet? Well, of course, I would look at UGLE first to see what it says about my country.

That's what I would do today. Some 30 years ago, however, I would not have had this chance...

But what would others do?

---

[1] http://bessel.org/exclartl.htm

Probably all those who are not so informed would choose a gate closer to home, let's say, or the first one that comes their way because they have friends who have already entered it.

They might find out, also from friends, that everything is exquisite there, that the Ritual is the same as at any other Lodge in this world, that all the Brethren are extraordinary, that they feel good together, and so on...

Those who would like to knock on that Gate have, at that moment, no way to know more. Besides, here too, the problems are more complicated and, why not put it bluntly: more serious.

Perhaps they will never find out that, although they enter an organism where everything seems to be regular, '*legitimate*', as UGLE expresses itself today, the truth.

For those at any Regular Grand Lodge on Earth will not recognize them, nor will someone even receive them when trying to visit any Grand Regular Lodge abroad, or even from their Homeland!

Not to mention that, above all, there are also '*clandestine*' or even '*wild*' lodges! These are Lodges or even Grand Lodges unrecognized by any other Grand Lodge, neither regular nor irregular.

In other words, these organizations work with no right, authority, or legitimate descent.

If you have the misfortune to knock on the door of a clandestine organization, you will become a Mason of this kind, that is, a clandestine one.

It doesn't sound right to be called a clandestine Mason, does it?

All Kinds of Gates...

Depending on one's luck or bad luck, one may find oneself at some point, unique in life, in fact, in front of a Gate that opens to GOOD or LESSER GOOD.

Maybe it's also about the effort made in understanding the importance of this unique step in a man's life and there is no discrimination here. These are the rules established in Freemasonry over 300 years ago and ready!

If you don't inform yourself, if you don't want to know more about what you should do at that one moment in your life, chances are you will be wrong.

Today, when the Internet can give you almost any answer, it is your mistake to knock on the wrong gate!

What could say those who have chosen another path?

They found themselves in an irregular lodge. Maybe they didn't even choose that Lodge. They did not know what means to be recognized worldwide by UGLE, to be clear to us why it is Regular.

With great enthusiasm, they were trying to explain to me exactly how they were told there too, inside:

You see… Things are not like that, that, in fact…'

And so on…

It's all About Knowing how to Knock on the Right Gate

Yes, that's right, and it's very easy to say. It's harder to do things the way you should.

This reminds me of the time I chose the Gate, about 30 years ago.

No one knew anything about others, who were also Brothers, like them, but they were on the Other Side. There was no Internet and you could not find such discreet information in the newspapers.

Maybe it would be more accurate to say that then the Gate was shown to me, rather…

The Man also Matters, not only the Gate

First, I met *Baronet Kapri*, the man who guided my first steps in Freemasonry.

I had countless philosophical discussions with him, which were not necessarily related to Freemasonry.

Everything in a spirit of immense openness, of close friendship, of brotherhood, before becoming Brethren.

In my time, only after months and months, I dared to ask if I could knock on the Gate too.

That's how I ended up being initiated.

The first time I was told about this step, about five years earlier, I didn't even dare think it could be me!

And now, looking back, I would say that I did well, very well, even. Those times were exaggeratedly turbulent, and just as exaggeratedly many were the inappropriate Paths.

Well, at that time, when there was no Internet, we were told that the *'others'* are not exactly good.

In fact, they were terrible. As we were told, the 'others' were doing I don't know what kind of odious things.

Also, of course, only *'we'* were the real ones, the good ones!

But after all, everything is fine when it ends even better!

---

*I've talked a lot about myself,
but I do it only so that others
wouldn't make my mistakes.*

*They can make their own
mistakes, after all!*

THINGS TO REMEMBER

There is only one Gate in one organization.

At several organizations, how could it be?

Everything is not as we would expect it to be when we talk of a serious and respectable organization such as Freemasonry, which is because its members are also human beings, after all.

The situation of the Grand Lodges, the situation on the ground, not from the height of UGLE, could be a little different...

Just like any good Mason I would like to be, I always expect to be corrected, so I can straighten up, of course.

Probably all those who are not so informed would choose a gate closer to home, let's say, or the first one that comes their way because they have friends who have already entered it.

If you have the misfortune to knock on the door of a clandestine organization, you will become a Mason of this kind, that is, a clandestine one.

Today, when the Internet can give you almost any answer, it is your mistake to knock on the wrong gate!

> In my time, only after months and months, I dared
> to ask if I could knock on the Gate too.

> I've talked a lot about myself, but I do it only so
> that others wouldn't make my mistakes.
> They can make their own mistakes, after all!

WHERE COULD BE MY PLACE?

Is There Room for me Too?

his is a question that anyone who thinks Freemasonry is for him too, should ask himself. To assume that we do not see an extra man in a crowd is a big mistake because Freemasonry is not a crowd...

Of course, if you are already 18 years old, you are eligible, according to UGLE rules.

It doesn't matter where you come from. You may come from a lost village in some distant mountains or the very center of the city.

We are talking here about an organization open to EVERYONE of this age and did not consider the fact that you are a billionaire, a country boy, or a star.

The purpose of Freemasonry, if not clear until now, is:

> 'to empower members to be the best they can be - it's about building character, supporting members as individuals, and helping them make a positive contribution to society.'[1]

This is what UGLE says, from the very beginning, specifying also, I would say, why Freemasonry is not just a certain crowd.

---

[1] https://www.ugle.org.uk/

It is up to everyone to understand if it may be his place there, in the Lodge.

> **Freemasonry provides a structure for members to come together under these common goals, enabling people to make new friendships, develop themselves and make valuable contributions to charitable causes.[2]**

Recognition, the UGLE Stamp?

All those who are not recognized as regulars by UGLE, the Grand Mother Lodge of the World, challenge this right or monopoly, as some say.

When you do not have UGLE recognition, you might try to explain/claim that it could be a mistake, because you do everything by the book, so...

Let's see what Regularity means, as already stated in 1929 the Board of General Purposes of UGLE in *'Basic Principles of Freemasonry'*:

---

[2] https://www.ugle.org.uk/

> 1. 1. Regularity of origin; i.e. each Grand Lodge shall have been established lawfully by a duly recognized Grand Lodge or by three or more regularly constituted Lodges.[3]

On the other hand, many do not want to believe that UGLE should decide for the whole of Earth.

Even though modern Freemasonry appeared a long time ago in London, they believe that this would not be a reason to have a monopoly. So, there are voices that say something like this:

> But why should the Grand Lodge of England have the privilege of 'saying regularity'?
>
> And if, unfortunately, and because the Great Architect does not want it, it becomes 'irregular', how will anyone know?[4]

Nowadays, conditions are different. We have plenty of information. Therefore, you can't believe that you could take another wrong step. Apparently, of course...

We may see that new Lodges, new Grand Lodges, new Federations, Unions, and Confederations are emerging.

---

[3] BASIC PRINCIPLES FOR GRAND LODGE RECOGNITION, Accepted by the Grand Lodge, September 4, 1929

[4] GUILLY, RENE, Renaissance Traditionnelle 17-18 (1974), p. 57

They do not even care about that Regularity given by the UGLE recognition.

These Masonic bodies recognize each other but among themselves.

They generously offer recognition to each other, create international organizations, and, of course, do not need UGLE to do so.

We could raise the issue of the principle of territoriality because there cannot theoretically be two Grand Lodges in the same country.

Yes, even in the UK there are other Grand Lodges, even older than UGLE!

To make things even more complicated, we also have Lodges that do not take into account any rules, the clandestine ones for real, so to speak.

They are not part of any Grand Lodge, not even one of those created clandestinely.

And yet, unfortunately, they attract many more or less innocent people.

Unfortunately, we can always see this happening again and again.

Just some Victims of Ambiguity?

Let's talk about the fact that in the age of practically instant searches on *Google*, there are still people who can be deceived, practically, by some well-crafted words of some well-done PR campaign.

I truly doubt that there could be any clandestine Lodge that would have made a Masonic temple the size of a huge cathedral. Even if so, it would catch the eye of anyone who sees it and feels the urgent need to join it.

I would say this even though I know cases that would be very similar to this scenario. For certain reasons that are easy to understand, because they are not the subject of this book, not for who knows what other reasons, I will pretend not to see them.

Let us never forget that this book speaks more than others about things that, in general, are exceptions, more or less common in Freemasonry.

This does not mean that we should avoid their problems, but rather that we should highlight them responsibly.

I said that I don't think there are such Lodges because a real construction, not some improvisation, would undoubtedly require a lot of money and, above all, would require substantial amounts of money to be thrown away.

*Our job is, as people of good faith,
not to let others fall into error.*

So, in general, if you don't rely on something, it's clear that you won't even start building a Masonic Temple, in vain and on your own money...

The Lodge as a Business

When you start such a business, because such a Lodge is mainly a business, you would make a plan, don't you?

I also drew attention to this aspect in my latest Masonic book: 'NEW MILLENNIUM MASONIC ETIQUETTE'.

Although a few years have passed since then, nothing has changed, because it's not just a problem belonging to these times. It's an old one.

And this issue is also about money.

This 'Lodge-business' is about a lot of money. Not just a small amount.

This business has to grow and grow smoothly!

We're talking here about money taken from some naïve persons by deception, to be clear. The victims are chosen professionally, we could say, from those who can pay more without too much trouble.

Almost 100 years ago, things were like this:

> Clandestine Masonry of today is wholly profit-making, begun and carried on by individuals who have nothing but duplicity to sell to their victims.
>
> Unfortunately, many honest men have been persuaded to pay fees for the 'degrees' of such spurious organizations, in the innocent belief that they were becoming regular Masons.
>
> Some pathetic cases form a part of the literature of clandestinism. [5]

What we can easily assume is that such a scheme should work smoothly, otherwise there would not be so many Lodges of this kind.

What we can easily assume is that such a scheme should work smoothly, otherwise there would not be so many Lodges of this kind.

Those impresarios, so to speak, namely those good people who took the money from these naïve

---

[5] SHORT TALK BULLETIN - Vol. XIII, December, 1935, No.12

persons, were aware since the beginning that this would be a trick that could work.

Indeed, there is still a small possibility, but which must be taken into account, that Regular Freemasonry may react.

We are talking here about a Regular Lodge, recognized by UGLE, to be clearer.

This Lodge may at some point conclude that it would be nice to receive generously in its ranks those who have been practically lost.

And, look, everyone is happy, no one remembers how the story started.

A happy ending!

Moreover, these naive persons might consider it to be a kind of exaggeratedly enormous investment indeed.

But, lo-and-behold, they used the money given for something, still, isn't it?

> **The charity of Masonry, however, is usually extended to the honest victims of misrepresentation, and such 'Masons' may apply, and, if they can pass the ballot in a regular Lodge, their misfortune in innocently entering a clandestine body seldom acts as an**

objection to their receiving the blessings of genuine Masonry.[6]

---

[6] SHORT TALK BULLETIN - Vol. XIII, December, 1935, No.12

THINGS TO REMEMBER

It doesn't matter where you come from. You may come from a lost village in some distant mountains or at the very center of the city.

It is up to everyone to understand if it may be his place there, in the Lodge.

When you do not have UGLE recognition, you might try to explain/claim that it is could be a mistake, because you do everything by the book, so...

We may see that new Lodges, new Grand Lodges, new Federations, Unions, and Confederations are emerging.
They do not even care about that regularity given by the UGLE recognition.

Yes, even in the UK there are other Grand Lodges, even older than UGLE!

Let us never forget that this book speaks more than others about things that, in general, are exceptions, more or less common in Freemasonry.

Our job is, as people of good faith, not to let others fall into error.

When you start such a business, because such a
  Lodge is mainly a business, you would make a
  plan, don't you?

This 'Lodge-business' is about a lot of money. Not
  just a small amount.
This business has to grow and grow smoothly!

And, look, everyone is happy, no one remembers
  how the story started.

A happy ending!

AT THE END OF THE WORLD

The Benefits of Freemasonry

 ooking beyond the Gate, you tend to believe that there must be some benefits. You think as a human being, after all. Otherwise, why would you want to enter Freemasonry?

Anyone looking for immediate, material benefits, especially as soon as he joins the Craft, should know that he has knocked on the wrong Gate.

After all, there are so many clubs, such as Lyons, for example. This might be more appropriate for the idea of socializing with others looking for just new business connections.

Here, in Freemasonry, only you have to win. Your business is something else. It doesn't belong to the world of a Masonic Temple.

Just as your religion doesn't matter, for example. What matters, instead, is to be Man, nothing more, but Man, with a big 'M'!

Do you want to be a better man?

Do you want to be with people who lead exemplary life?

Do you want to help the weakest?

Then, yes, this is the Gate to knock on!

What Could Freemasonry Offer You?

One of the most important effects of Masonic Life is to encourage study for your perfection as a Man.

This could include, besides everything related to the Masonic esoteric, for example:

- *Improving and, (why not?), correcting your vocabulary;*
- *A greater interest in knowing history;*
- *Increasing interest in the study, in general.*

By speaking in front of several people, even in front of the Brethren from his Lodge, the Mason would gain, over time, self-confidence and more public speaking skills, such as:

- *Ease of public speaking;*
- *Gaining and refining debate skills;*
- *Improving rhetoric.*

Looking at what his Brethren do, the Freemason can cultivate his leadership skills, going through various functions, from the lowest to the highest, culminating in that of the leader of the Lodge, namely the *Worshipful Master.*

He learns the importance of humility, understands how to do as much as he can for charity, and, more than that, values the need to give back something of yourself.

Freemasonry provides you with an adequate framework for perfecting the inherent skills already present in you.

Between two Worlds...

We all live between two worlds, the real one and the one we think we live in.

The real world is one where you can sell and buy anything, even people, because many of them are for sale, with or without their knowledge.

You don't even have to look for them too long to buy them. You may find them everywhere, with a sign that reads 'FOR SALE.'

They have no chance of becoming true Masons, although this is only ideal, unfortunately. There are a few already inside because Freemasonry is a group of people, not saints, and I said this before.

Theoretically, as the Old Masonic Teachings say, things are like this:

Freemasonry strives to teach us we can become better people, better children, better parents, better friends, better citizens.

And so it should be!

If you respect the basic principles of Freemasonry, all the Teachings, then it will be so, after all!

THINGS TO REMEMBER

Anyone looking for immediate, material benefits,
especially as soon as he joins the Craft,
should know that he has knocked on the
wrong Gate.

Do you want to be a better man?
Do you want to be with people who lead
exemplary life?
Do you want to help the weakest?
Then, yes, this is the Gate to knock on!

Freemasonry provides you with an adequate
framework for perfecting the inherent skills
already present in you.

We all live between two worlds, the real one and
the one we think we live in.

Freemasonry strives to teach us we can become
better people, better children, better parents,
better friends, better citizens.

If you respect the basic principles of
Freemasonry, all the Teachings, then it will be
so, after all!

AT THE END OF THE BOOK

What Should We Do?

We might like to know what we could do with the new Freemasonry and its new members. If we could have a solution, immediately, Heaven would be ours!?

Unfortunately, we don't have the answers. We can only ask questions everyone can answer as they learned: by looking in the mirror...

Freemasonry should be full only of people who are examples to others around them.

This is an ideal scenario, of course.

It depends, now, on what kind of examples might be, after all...

What seems to be more important is that everyone seeks solutions to their problems concerning Freemasonry. In principle, they should be spiritual concerns.

Also, in principle, they could solve the problems by reading the Masonic Teachings. Nothing should be an obstacle. Maybe only that *Ego* we always blame...

It could be difficult to make peace between the world in the Temple, the world outside, and, why not, the world within us.

But we have to try if that's the reason for joining Freemasonry.

If we came in for something else, for alleged material advantages, then there is nothing to do or discuss. It's a long way from material thinking to spiritual thinking...

The Tentacles of the Outside World

Just as water rushes everywhere, so do the tentacles of the imperfect world from the outside right inside the Masonic Temple.

As murky as the pouring water, the misery of the outside world, beyond the doors of the Temple, a world full of envy and hatred, with endless armed conflicts between people of different religious beliefs or not, swirls over the silence of the Temple.

Perhaps, it might not at all be easy to follow the moral principles of Freemasonry in everyday life. Maybe it doesn't seem *'cool'* at all.

But, if you don't throw your cigarette from the window of your luxury car, you won't be any worse or sillier than the scumbags who do.

It is the choice of each of us, his free will, to be as he thinks it might be better. We don't have to worry, because there is Somebody to judge him, not us.

We should never forget that Freemasonry is, through its members, a mirror of society.

For over 300 years, Freemasonry has imposed and maintained its high standards through the quality and deeds of its members.

He who enters Freemasonry must first be a worthy man, then be worthy to be a Freemason, a member of a Brotherhood of worthy people.

Even You Are a Mason?

There have always been all kinds of people, better, worse, who became Freemasons.

Not all of them were role models, neither in the beginning nor later.

But this is the status quo. Freemasonry comprises people, subject to mistakes.

Therefore, as human beings, we, the ones who understand this, must do everything in our power to change things for the better.

We, those who understand this,
have a duty to be different...

Maybe then we won't have the opportunity to hear a question that sounds something like this:

- *How come that even you are a Mason?*

In other words, did this honorable organization end up in such a way that it even received you in its ranks???

It is not at all honorable, neither for the one asked, nor for the other Masons, *'good Men and true, or Men of Honor and Honesty,'* as Anderson said.

However, I would like to end this book on a sincere note of hope: I would very much like to never hear such a question again!

For others, just a word of encouragement:

Let no Brother forget he is the mirror of Freemasonry...

Most of all, perhaps,
as Freemasons, we have to be
honorable citizens anytime,
anywhere, regardless of those
around us.

And it will be better for all of us.

THINGS TO REMEMBER

Freemasonry should be full only of people who are examples to others around them.

It could be difficult to make peace between the world in the Temple, the world outside, and, why not, the world within us.

Just as water rushes everywhere, so do the tentacles of the imperfect world from the outside right inside the Masonic Temple.

It is the choice of each of us, his free will, to be as he thinks it might be better.

He who enters Freemasonry must first be a worthy man, then be worthy to be a Freemason, a member of a Brotherhood of worthy people.

But this is the status quo.
Freemasonry comprises people, subject to mistakes.

We, those who understand this, have a duty to be different.

Most of all, perhaps, as Freemasons, we have to be honorable citizens anytime, anywhere, regardless of those around us.

And it will be better for all of us.

ESSENTIAL DOCUMENTS

CHARGES OF A FREE-MASON

CHARGES OF A FREE-MASON,
EXTRACTED FROM
The Ancient RECORDS of LODGES
beyond Sea, and of those in *England, Scotland,* and *Ireland,* for the Use of the Lodges.

TO BE READ
At The Making of NEW BRETHREN, or when the *MASTER* shall order it.

I. Concerning GOD and RELIGION.

A *Mason* is obliged by his Tenure, to obey the moral Law; and if he rightly understands the Art, he will never be a stupid Atheist nor an irreligious **Libertine**. But though in ancient Times *Masons* were charged in every Country to be of the Religion of that Country or Nation, whatever it was, yet 'tis now thought more expedient only to oblige them to that Religion in which all Men agree, leaving their particular Opinions to themselves; that is, to be *good* Men and *true*, or Men of Honour and Honesty, by whatever Denominations or Persuasions they may be distinguished; whereby Masonry becomes the *Center of Union*, and the Means of conciliating true Friendship among Persons that must have remained at a perpetual Distance.

II. Of the CIVIL MAGISTRATES supreme and subordinate.

A *Mason* is a peaceable Subject to the Civil Powers, wherever he resides or works, and is never to be concerned in Plots and Conspiracies against the Peace and Welfare of the

Nation, nor to behave himself undutifully to inferior Magistrates; for as Masonry hath been always injured by War, Bloodshed, and Confusion, so ancient Kings and Princes have been much disposed to encourage the Craftsmen, because of their Peaceableness and *Loyalty*, whereby they practically answered the Cavils of their Adversaries, and promoted the Honour of the Fraternity, who ever flourished in Times of Peace. So that if a Brother should be a Rebel against the State he is not to be countenanced in his Rebellion, however he may be pitied as an unhappy Man; and, if convicted of no other Crime though the loyal Brotherhood must and ought to disown his Rebellion, and give no Umbrage or Ground of political Jealousy to the Government for the time being; they cannot expel him from the *Lodge*, and his Relation to it remains indefeasible.

III.   Of LODGES.

A LODGE is a place where *Masons* assemble and work: Hence that Assembly, or duly organized Society of *Masons*, is called a LODGE, and every Brother ought to belong to one, and to be subject to its *By-Laws* and the GENERAL REGULATIONS. It is either *particular* or *general*, and will be best understood by attending it, and by the Regulations of the *General* or *Grand Lodge hereunto annexed. In ancient Times, no Master or Fellow could be absent from it especially when warned to appear at it, without incurring a sever Censure, until it appeared to the Master and Wardens that pure Necessity hindered him.*

The persons admitted Members of a Lodge must be good and true Men, free-born, and of mature and discreet Age, no Bondmen no Women, no immoral or scandalous men, but of good Report.

IV. Of Masters, WARDENS, Fellows and Apprentices.

All preferment among Masons is grounded upon real Worth and personal Merit only; that so the Lords may be well served, the Brethren not put to Shame, nor the Royal Craft despised: Therefore no Master or Warden is chosen by Seniority, but for his Merit. It is impossible to describe these things in Writing, and every Brother must attend in his Place, and learn them in a way peculiar to this Fraternity: Only Candidates may know that no Master should take an Apprentice unless he has sufficient Employment for him, and unless he be a perfect Youth having no Maim or Defect in his Body that may render him incapable of learning the Art of serving his Master's LORD, and of being made a Brother, and then a Fellow-Craft in due time, even after he has served such a Term of Years as the Custom of the Country directs; and that he should be descended of honest Parents; that so, when otherwise qualified he may arrive to the Honour of being the WARDEN, and then the Master of the Lodge, the Grand Warden, and at length the GRAND MASTER of all the Lodges, according to his Merit.

No Brother can be a WARDEN until he has passed the part of a Fellow-Craft; nor a MASTER until he has acted as a Warden, nor GRAND WARDEN until he has been Master of a Lodge, nor Grand Master unless he has been a Fellow-Craft before his Election, who is also to be nobly born, or a Gentleman of the best Fashion, or some eminent Scholar, or some curious Architect, or other Artist, descended of honest Parents, and who is of similar great Merit in the Opinion of the Lodges. And for the better, and easier, and more honourable Discharge of his Office, the Grand-Master has a Power to choose his own DEPUTY GRAND-MASTER, who must be then, or must have been formerly, the Master of a particular Lodge, and has the Privilege of acting whatever the GRAND MASTER, his Principal, should act, unless the said Principal be present, or interpose his Authority by a Letter

These Rulers and Governors, supreme and subordinate, of the ancient Lodge, are to be obeyed in their respective Stations by all the Brethren, according to the old Charges and Regulations, with all Humility, Reverence, Love and Alacrity.

V.   Of the Management of the CRAFT in working.

All Masons shall work honestly on working Days, that they may live creditably on holy Days; and the time appointed by the Law of the Land or confirmed by Custom, shall be observed.

The most expert of the Fellow-Craftsmen shall be chosen or appointed the Master or Overseer of the Lord's Work; who is to be called MASTER by those that work under him. The Craftsmen are to avoid all ill Language, and to call each other by no disobliging Name, but Brother or Fellow; and to behave themselves courteously within and without the Lodge. The Master, knowing himself to be able of Cunning, shall undertake the Lord's Work as reasonably as possible, and truly dispend his Goods as if they were his own; nor to give more Wages to any Brother or Apprentice than he really may deserve.

Both the Master and the Masons receiving their Wages justly, shall be faithful to the Lord and honestly finish their Work, whether Task or journey; nor put the work to Task that hath been accustomed to Journey.

None shall discover Envy at the Prosperity of a Brother, nor supplant him, or put him out of his Work, if he be capable to finish the same; for no Man can finish another's Work so much to the Lord's Profit, unless he be thoroughly acquainted with the Designs and Draughts of him that began it.

When a Fellow-Craftsman is chosen Warden of the Work under the Master, he shall be true both to Master and Fellows, shall carefully oversee the Work in the Master's Absence to the Lord's profit; and his Brethren shall obey him.

All Masons employed shall meekly receive their Wages without Murmuring or Mutiny, and not desert the Master till the Work is finished.

A younger Brother shall be instructed in working, to prevent spoiling the Materials for want of Judgment, and for increasing and continuing of Brotherly Love.

All the Tools used in working shall be approved by the Grand Lodge.

No Labourer shall be employed in the proper Work of Masonry; nor shall Free Masons work with those that are not free, without an urgent Necessity; nor shall they teach Labourers and unaccepted Masons as they should teach a Brother or Fellow.

VI.   Of BEHAVIOUR, VIZ.

1. In the Lodge while constituted.

You are not to hold private Committees, or separate Conversation without Leave from the Master, nor to talk of anything impertinent or unseemly, nor interrupt the Master or Wardens, or any Brother speaking to the Master: Nor behave yourself ludicrously or jestingly while the Lodge is engaged in what is serious and solemn; nor use any unbecoming Language upon any Pretense whatsoever; but to pay due Reverence to your Master, Wardens, and Fellows, and put them to worship.

If any Complaint be brought, the Brother found guilty shall stand to the Award and Determination of the Lodge, who are the proper and competent Judges of all such Controversies (unless you carry it by Appeal to the GRAND LODGE), and to whom they ought to be referred, unless a Lord's Work be hindered the mean while, in which Case a particular Reference may be made; but you must never go to Law about what concerneth Masonry, without an absolute necessity apparent to the Lodge.

2.   **Behaviour** after the LODGE is over and the Brethren not gone.

You may enjoy yourself with innocent Mirth, treating one another according to Ability, but avoiding all Excess, or forcing any Brother to eat or drink beyond his Inclination, or hindering him from going when his Occasions call him, or doing or saying anything offensive, or that may forbid an easy and free Conversation, for that would blast our Harmony,and defeat our laudable Purposes. Therefore no private Piques or Quarrels must be brought within the Door of the Lodge, far less any Quarrels about Religion, or Nations, or State Policy, we being only, as Masons, we are also of all Nations, Tongues, Kindreds, and Languages, and are resolved against all Politics, as what never yet conducted to the Welfare of the Lodge, nor ever will. This Charge has been always strictly enjoined and observed.

3.   **Behaviour** when Brethren meet without Strangers, but not in a Lodge formed.

You are to salute one another in a courteous Manner, as you will be instructed, calling each other Brother, freely giving mutual instruction as shall be thought expedient, without being ever seen or overheard, and without encroaching upon each other, or derogating from that Respect which is due to any Brother, were he not Mason: For though all Masons are as Brethren upon the same Level, yet Masonry takes no Honour from a man that he had before; nay, rather it adds to his Honour, especially if he has deserved well of the Brotherhood, who must give Honour to whom it is due, and avoid ill Manners.

4.   **Behaviour** in Presence of Strangers not Masons.

You shall be cautious in your Words and Carriage, that the most penetrating Stranger shall not be able to discover or find out what is not proper to be intimated, and sometimes you shall divert a Discourse, and manage it prudently for the Honour of the worshipful Fraternity.

5.   **Behaviour** at Home, and in your Neighbourhood.

You are to act as becomes a moral and wise Man; particularly not to let your Family, Friends and Neighbors know the Concern of the Lodge, &c., but wisely to consult your own

Honour, and that of the ancient Brotherhood, for reasons not to be mentioned here You must also consult your Health, by not continuing together too late, or too long from Home, after Lodge Hours are past; and by avoiding of Gluttony or Drunkenness, that your Families be not neglected or injured, nor you disabled from working.

6.   **Behaviour** towards a strange Brother.

You are cautiously to examine him, in such a Method as Prudence shall direct you, that you may not be imposed upon by an ignorant, false Pretender, whom you are to reject with Contempt and Derision, and beware of giving him any Hints of Knowledge.

But if you discover him to be a true and genuine Brother, you are to respect him accordingly; and if he is in want, you must relieve him if you can, or else direct him how he may be relieved: you must employ him some days, or else recommend him to be employed. But you are not charged to do beyond your Ability, only to prefer a poor Brother, that is a good Man and true before any other poor People in the same Circumstance.

Finally, All these Charges you are to observe, and also those that shall be recommended to you in another Way; cultivating BROTHERLY-LOVE, the Foundation and Cape-stone, the Cement and Glory of this Ancient Fraternity, avoiding all Wrangling and Quarreling, all Slander and Backbiting, nor permitting others to slander any honest Brother, but defending his Character, and doing him all good Offices, as far as is consistent with your Honour and Safety, and no farther. And if any of them do you Injury, you must apply to your own or his Lodge, and from thence you may appeal to the Grand Lodge, at the Quarterly Communication and from thence to the annual GRAND LODGE at the Quarterly Communication, and from thence to the annual GRAND LODGE, as has been the ancient laudable Conduct of our Fore-fathers in every Nation; never taking a legal Course but when the Case cannot be otherwise decided, and patiently listening to the honest and friendly Advice of Master and Fellows, when they would prevent your going to Law with Strangers, or would excite you to put a speedy Period to all Law-Suits, so that you may mind the Affair of MASONRY with the more Alacrity and Success; but with respect to Brothers or Fellows at Law, the Master and Brethren should kindly offer their Mediation, which ought to be thankfully submitted to by the contending Brethren; and if that submission is impracticable, they must, however, carry on their

Process, or Law-Suit, without Wrath and Rancor (not in the common way) saying or doing nothing which may hinder Brotherly Love, and good Offices to be renewed and continued; that all may see the benign Influence of MASONRY, as all true Masons have done from the beginning of the World, and will do to the End of Time.

Amen so mote it be.

SUMMARY OF THE ANTIENT CHARGES AND REGULATIONS

Summary of the
ANTIENT CHARGES AND REGULATIONS to be read by the Secretary (or acting Secretary), to the MASTER ELECT, prior to his Installation into the Chair of a Lodge.

1. You agree to be a good Man and true, and strictly to obey the moral law.

2. You are to be a peaceable Subject, and cheerfully to conform to the laws of the country in which you reside.

3. You promise not to be concerned in plots or Conspiracies against Government, but patiently to submit to the decisions of the Supreme Legislature.

4. You agree to pay a proper respect to the Civil Magistrate, to work diligently, live creditably, and act honourably by all Men.

5. You agree to hold in veneration the original Rulers and Patrons of the Order of Free-Masonry, and their regular Successors, supreme and subordinate, according to their Stations; and to submit to the Awards and Resolutions of your Brethren in general Lodge convened, in every case consistent with the Constitutions of the Order.

6. You agree to avoid private piques and quarrels and to guard against intemperance and excess.

7. You agree to be cautious in your carriage and behaviour, courteous to your Brethren, and faithful to your Lodge.

8. You promise to respect genuine and true Brethren, and to discountenance Impostors and all Dissenters from the original Plan of Free-Masonry.

9. You agree to promote the general good of Society, to cultivate the Social Virtues, and to propagate the knowledge of the Mystic Art as far as your influence and ability can extend.

10. You promise to pay homage to the Grand Master for the time being, and to his Officers when duly installed, and strictly to conform to every Edict of the Grand Lodge.

11. You admit that it is not in the power of any Man or Body of Men to make any Alteration or Innovation in the Body of Masonry without the consent first obtained of the Grand Lodge.

12.   You promise a regular attendance on the Communications and Committees of the Grand Lodge, upon receiving proper notice thereof, and to pay attention to all the duties of Free-Masonry upon proper and convenient occasions.

13.   You admit that no new Lodge can be formed without permission of the Grand Master or his Deputy, and that no countenance ought to be given to any irregular Lodge, or to any person initiated therein; and that no public processions of Masons clothed with the Badges of the Order can take place without the special Licence of the Grand Master or his Deputy.

14.   You admit that no person can regularly be made a Free-Mason or admitted a Member of any Lodge without previous notice and due inquiry into his character; and that no Brother can be advanced to a higher Degree except in strict conformity with the Laws of the Grand Lodge.

15.   You promise that no Visitor shall be received into your Lodge without due examination, and producing proper Vouchers of his having been initiated in a regular Lodge.

At the conclusion the Installing Officer addresses the Master Elect as follows: 'Do you submit to and promise to support these Charges and Regulations as Masters have done in all ages?' Upon his answering in the affirmative the Ceremony of Installation proceeds.

BASIC PRINCIPLES FOR GRAND LODGE RECOGNITION[1]

Accepted by the Grand Lodge, September 4, 1929

The M.W. The Grand Master having expressed a desire that the Board would draw up a statement of the Basic Principles on which this Grand Lodge could be invited to recognize any Grand Lodge applying for recognition by the English Jurisdiction, the Board of General Purposes has gladly complied. The result, as follows, has been approved by the Grand Master and it will form the basis of a questionnaire to be forwarded in future to each Jurisdiction requesting English recognition. The Board desires that not only such bodies but the Brethren generally throughout the Grand Master's Jurisdiction shall be fully informed as to those Basic Principles of Freemasonry for which the Grand Lodge of England has stood throughout its history

1. Regularity of origin; i.e. each Grand Lodge shall have been established lawfully by a duly recognized Grand Lodge or by three or more regularly constituted Lodges.

2. That a belief in the G.A.O.T.U. and His revealed will shall be an essential qualification for membership.

3. That all Initiates shall take their Obligation on or in full view of the open Volume of the Sacred Law, by which is meant the

---

[1] http://www.ugle.org.uk/images/files/Book_of_Constitutions_-_Craft_Rules_Sept_2017.pdf

revelation from above which is binding on the conscience of the particular individual who is being initiated.

4. That the membership of the Grand Lodge and individual Lodges shall be composed exclusively of men; and that each Grand Lodge shall have no Masonic intercourse of any kind with mixed Lodges or bodies which admit women to membership.

5. That the Grand Lodge shall have sovereign jurisdiction over the Lodges under its control; i.e. that it shall be a responsible, independent, self-governing organization, with sole and undisputed authority over the Craft or Symbolic Degrees (Entered Apprentice, Fellow Craft, and Master Mason) within its Jurisdiction; and shall not in any way be subject to, or divide such authority with, a Supreme Council or other Power claiming any control or supervision over those degrees.

6. That the three Great Lights of Freemasonry (namely, the Volume of the Sacred Law, the Square, and the Compasses) shall always be exhibited when the Grand Lodge or its subordinate Lodges are at work, the chief of these being the Volume of the Sacred Law.

7. That the discussion of religion and politics within the Lodge shall be strictly prohibited.

8. That the principles of the Antient Landmarks, customs, and usages of the Craft shall be strictly observed.

SELECTIVE BIBLIOGRAPHY

In order of appearance

- Matzota, Eugen, Masonic Etiquette in the New Millennium, Madrid, 2015;
- Matzota, Eugen, New Millennium Masonic Etiquette, 2019;
- Anderson, James, The Constitutions of the Free-Masons, THE CHARGES of a FREE-MASON, London, 1723
- GUILLY, RENE, Renaissance Traditionnelle 17-18 (1974)
- Pike, Albert, Morals and Dogma, 1871
- BASIC PRINCIPLES FOR GRAND LODGE RECOGNITION, Accepted by Grand Lodge, 4 September 1929
- Della Mirandola, Giovanni Pico, Oration on the Dignity of Man, 1486
- The Holy Bible, King James Version (KJV),
- SHORT TALK BULLETIN - Vol. XIII, December, 1935, No.12
- UGLE, Book of Constitutions

Web pages

- http://www.ugle.org.uk/images/files/Book_of_Constitutions_-_Craft_Rules_Sept_2017.pdf
- https://archive.org/stream/moralsdogmaofanc00pikeiala/moralsdogmaofanc00pikeiala_djvu.txt